25
Favorite
Stories
From The Bible

Stories by
Ura Miller

Illustrations by
Gloria Oostema

To obtain information or a catalog of publications, please contact:
TGS International
P.O. Box 355
Berlin, Ohio 44610, USA

TGS International is a wholly-owned subsidiary of Christian Aid Ministries, Berlin, Ohio.

This title is also available in Romanian, Russian, Ukrainian, Spanish, Haitian Creole, and German.

Library of Congress Catalog Cardnumber
94-075773

ISBN 978-1-885270-36-8

Printed in China

OLD TESTAMENT

Table of Contents

GOD'S WONDERFUL CREATION
In the Beginning

The Holy Bible begins with God. He created the beautiful heavens above, and the earth below for us to live on. There was a time when everything was dark, very dark. No birds, animals, or laughter of little children were heard.

Then a voice spoke: "Let there be light!" And suddenly there was light! God separated the light from the darkness and named them day and night. This happened the very first day.

On the second day, God started to make a beautiful world. He divided the water from the air. Then the blue sky appeared.

On the third day, God made dry land by gathering the waters into oceans, streams, and rivers. He covered the plains, hills, and mountains with grass, flowers, vines, and trees. Olives, apples, cherries, peaches, and berries grew on trees and bushes.

On the fourth day, God put something yellow and round in the sky. It was the sun. In the evening a glowing moon appeared, and many stars dotted the sky.

On the fifth day, there were sounds everywhere. What did God create this day? He made birds to fly in the air and fish to swim in the water. They were all sizes, shapes, and colors. Whales, goldfish, bluebirds, geese, and ostriches were only a few of the many creatures He made.

On the sixth day, cattle, creeping things, and other animals were seen. God made cows, horses, sheep, dogs, and cats, along with lions, tigers, bears, and rabbits. It was a wonderful birthday present for the very first man whom God also created that day. Do you know the name of this first man? In the next story, you will read about him.

On the seventh day, God rested. He called it a Holy Day, for He had finished all His good work.

Genesis 1; 2:1-3

God created a wonderful world.

Parents: *Through faith we understand that the worlds were framed by the word of God.* (Hebrews 11:3)

Children: 1. Who made all things that live?
2. Can you name some nice things that God made?
3. How many days did it take God to create the world?

ADAM AND EVE
The First Man and the Mother of All Living

On the sixth day of creation, God's world was beautiful indeed. The fields were green, the flowers bloomed, and birds and animals roamed the forests.

But there were no people, houses, farms, or cities on the earth. No children played under the trees. The world was ready for men and women to enjoy it.

God said, "Let us make man in our likeness. He will have a soul and be master of all that is on the earth."

Then God took dust from the earth and formed a man. He breathed into him the breath of life, and the man became a living soul. God named this very first man *Adam*.

To give man a home, God planted a beautiful garden in Eden with a clear river flowing through it. Adam was to care for this garden. Then God brought the animals to Adam and let him name each one. Adam noticed there were two of every kind of animal.

But there was no companion for Adam in this perfect garden. God said, "It is not good for the man to be alone. I will make someone to be with Adam and to help him."

God caused Adam to fall into a deep sleep, then He took a rib from Adam's side. From the rib, God made a woman. Adam called her *Eve*. Adam and Eve loved each other. They were very happy in this beautiful garden God had given them for a home.

Genesis 1:26; 2

Adam and Eve in the beautiful Garden of Eden.

Parents: *I will praise thee; for I am fearfully and wonderfully made.*
(Psalm 139:14)

Children: 1. Who made Adam and Eve?
2. Who named the animals that God made?
3. In what garden did Adam and Eve live?

THE FIRST SIN
Cast Out of the Garden of Eden

For a time—we do not know how long—Adam and Eve were at peace in their beautiful garden. They talked with God as a man would talk with his friend. They did whatever God told them to and did not know of anything evil.

Yet Adam and Eve needed to learn that they must always obey God's commands. God told Adam and Eve, "You may eat the fruit from all the trees in the garden except one. If you eat the fruit of that tree, you will die."

Now among the animals there was a serpent, or a snake. Satan, that evil spirit who tempts us to sin, went into the serpent to tempt the woman to sin.

The serpent said to Eve, "You will not die. God knows that if you eat of the fruit, you will become very wise and know what is good and what is evil."

Eve listened to the serpent. She looked at the fruit, thought of how good it would taste, and wondered if it would really make her wise. Ignoring God's command, she took the fruit and ate it. Then she gave some to Adam, and he also ate.

That evening when Adam and Eve heard God's voice, they did not come to Him as before. Fearfully they tried to hide.

Because of their disobedience, God said to Eve, "You will suffer pain and trouble, and your husband will rule over you." To Adam, God said, "Because you listened to your wife when she told you to do wrong, you, too, must suffer by toiling and sweating among thorns and thistles." God also cursed the serpent.

Adam and Eve could not stay in their perfect garden home. God sent them out and placed angels and a flaming sword at the entrance.

Genesis 3

Adam and Eve sent out of the garden because of disobedience.

Parents: *For as by one man's disobedience many were made sinners, so by the obedience of one shall many be made righteous.* (Romans 5:19)

Children:
1. Who tempted Eve?
2. Why did Adam and Eve hide from God?
3. Who made Adam and Eve leave the garden?

NOAH—THE ARK BUILDER
History's First Boat Ride

After a long while, there were many people on the earth. Sad to say, they had become very wicked. God decided to destroy them by sending a flood.

As God looked down from heaven, He saw one good man called Noah. Because Noah was God's friend, God told him about the flood He was going to send. He commanded Noah to build a big ark, and told him exactly how to do it.

No doubt the wicked people laughed at Noah for building this great boat when there was no water for it to float on. But Noah kept right on building as God had commanded. He believed God's Word. Noah also preached to the people about God and the punishment that was coming.

Finally the ark was finished, more than one hundred years later. God told Noah to come into the ark with his family of eight. God caused animals, birds, and creeping things to enter the ark so that some of every kind could be kept alive. When they were all safe inside, God shut the door.

After seven days, it began to rain. It rained forty days and forty nights without stopping. Rain fell as if it were poured out of great windows in the heavens. Water flooded the whole earth until there was no dry ground or breath of life left on it.

High above the earth floated the ark with Noah and his family. After many days the water began to go down, and the ark bumped onto the mountains of Ararat. One day Noah opened the window of the ark and sent out a dove. But the dove came back because it could not find a dry place to stay. A week later, Noah sent out the dove again. This time it returned with a leaf in its beak. The water must be below the trees by now! The next time he sent out the dove, it did not come back. Then Noah knew the earth had become dry again.

God called Noah and his family out of the ark. Noah was so thankful to God for saving their lives that he built an altar of worship. There God formed a beautiful rainbow in the sky. He told Noah that it was a sign of His promise never again to destroy the earth with a flood.

Genesis 6; 7; 8; 9:1-18

Noah and his family thank God for saving their lives.

Parents: *For thou art not a God that hath pleasure in wickedness: neither shall evil dwell with thee.* (Psalm 5:4)

Children: 1. Who told Noah to build an ark?
2. What was in the ark besides Noah and his family?
3. Why did God place a rainbow in the sky?

TOWER OF BABEL
The Beginning of Different Languages

The great flood that God had sent soon became a dim memory in the minds of Noah's children. Their families continued to grow until there were many people in the world. But the thoughts of their hearts were again becoming evil.

As people traveled from the east, they found some level land. At that time all the people spoke the same language. They said to each other, "Let us make bricks and bake them thoroughly. Then let us build a big city with a very high tower in it. We will make a name for ourselves so that we will never be scattered."

They began to build the city and the tower. But the Lord came down from heaven to see this thing, and it displeased Him very much.

God caused men to speak different languages which they had never spoken before. The builders could not finish their city and tower because they were not able to understand each other anymore. They stopped the work and began spreading apart into other lands. The unfinished city was named *Babel*, a word meaning *confusion*. Ever since that time, many languages are spoken on the earth.

As time went on, more and more people prayed to images of wood and stone called idols. They thought these images were gods that could hear their prayers and help them. These people did not call on the true God or know His will. They did many evil things.

But the Lord God saw a different kind of man in the city of Ur. This man, Abram, prayed to the Lord and always tried to do His will, even though wicked people lived all around him. The Lord said, "Abram, go away from this place. Leave your father's house and go to a place that I will show you. I will bless you and make you a blessing to others." Abram obeyed God, even though he did not understand.

Genesis 10; 11:1-9

The city and tower of Babel being built.

Parents: *He hath showed strength with his arm; he hath scattered the proud in the imagination of their hearts.* (Luke 1:51)

Children:
1. Was God pleased that the people were building the tower of Babel?
2. What did He do to stop them from building?
3. What did God tell Abram to do?

13

ABRAM AND LOT
Sodom is Destroyed

Abram took his wife, Sara, and his tents, sheep, cattle, and servants, and left his home in Ur. His nephew Lot, who also had animals and tents, went with them. They crossed rivers and climbed hills until at last they came into the land of Canaan. This was the land God had told Abram about.

They set up their tents and prepared to live there. Every morning, the herdsmen took the livestock out to pasture, but they soon ran into a problem. There was not enough land for all the animals. Abram and Lot would have to separate.

"You may choose whether to go or stay," Abram told Lot.

Lot looked toward the city of Sodom. The land around it was beautiful with green grass and plenty of water. He chose the best land and moved his animals and possessions to Sodom.

One day, a while later, three men came to Abram and told him that God was going to destroy Sodom because the people were so wicked. These men were angels from God. One big sin of Sodom was that men married men and women married women. God wants one man to marry one woman. But the people of Sodom did not care about God's law.

Abram pleaded with God to spare Sodom. God agreed that if ten righteous people could be found in Sodom, He would not destroy the city. But not even ten people loved God.

Lot was sitting in the city gate when the angels arrived in Sodom. He welcomed the visitors and took them home with him for the night. The angels warned Lot that God would destroy the city. The next morning they said, "Hurry, take your wife and your daughters, and get out of the city." They quickly led Lot and his wife and daughters out of the city, warning the small group not to look back.

Then the Lord sent fire and brimstone out of heaven and burned up the city of Sodom and the land around it. Lot's wife could not resist looking back, and she was turned into a pillar of salt.

What a sad story. Lot selfishly chose the most beautiful land and ended up losing his wife and home. God wants us to stay away from evil. It is His will that one man marries one woman. God will judge people who do not do right. But those who obey God, like Abram did, will be blessed.

Genesis 12; 13; 18; 19

Faithful Abram takes his family to the land of Canaan.

Parents: *By faith Abraham, when he was called to go out into a place which he should after receive for an inheritance, obeyed; and he went out, not knowing whither he went.* (Hebrews 11:8)

Children: 1. To what land did Abram take his wife and Lot?
2. Who chose the best land? Where was it?
3. Why did God destroy Sodom?

ABRAHAM'S SACRIFICE
A Great Test of Love

The Lord came to Abram and said, "I will give this land to your children, and to their children, and it will be their land forever." Abram built an altar and made an offering to the Lord and worshiped Him.

Another time, God told Abram, "Can you count the stars? Neither will you be able to count your descendants." Abram believed God would give him many descendants even though he had no children yet. Later God changed Abram's name to Abraham, which means *father of a multitude*. He promised to give Abraham and his wife Sarah a son, a people, and a land. Abraham promised to serve God faithfully.

One day three strangers came to Abraham's tent door. By this time Abraham was one hundred years old and Sarah ninety years old. The strangers told Abraham that Sarah would have a son. Sarah overheard it and laughed to herself, "How can I have a child when I am so old?"

But the men, who were angels sent by God, said, "Is anything too hard for the Lord?"

Finally the promised child indeed was born to Abraham and Sarah. They named him *Isaac*, as the Lord had told them to. They were very happy to have a little boy.

Then one day God said to Abraham, "Take now your only son, whom you love, and go to a mountain which I will show you. Offer him there for a burnt offering."

Though the command filled Abraham's heart with pain, he began to obey at once. With two servants and a donkey, Abraham and Isaac started northward.

On the third day, Abraham and young Isaac went up on the mountain by themselves. There Abraham built an altar. He placed the wood in order, tied Isaac, and laid him on it. At last he raised his knife to kill his son.

Just then the angel of the Lord called, "Abraham, do not hurt your son Isaac! Now I know you love God more than your son." What joy and relief those heavenly words brought to Abraham!

Then Abraham turned and saw a ram caught by its horns in the bushes. How thankful Abraham was to offer the ram instead of his son.

Genesis 15:1-6; 21; 22

Abraham is thankful that he does not have to offer his son.

Parents: *He that loveth son or daughter more than me is not worthy of me.* (Matthew 10:37b)

Children: 1. What does the name *Abraham* mean?
              2. How old was Abraham when Isaac was born?
              3. Why do you think God asked Abraham to sacrifice his son?

JACOB RECEIVES THE BLESSING
Esau Sells His Birthright

After Abraham died, God was very kind to Isaac and blessed him. However, Isaac's wife Rebekah had no children for nineteen years. Isaac prayed earnestly for a child, and God answered his prayer.

Twin boys, Esau and Jacob, were born to Isaac and Rebekah. Esau grew up to be a hunter. He was rough and covered with hair. Jacob was quiet and thoughtful. He stayed at home and took care of his father's flocks. Isaac loved Esau more than Jacob, because he liked the deer meat that Esau brought him. But Rebekah loved Jacob more.

In those days, the oldest son in every family had what was called the birthright. This made him the chief among all the children, and he received a special blessing. Esau, as the older, had a "birthright" to more of Isaac's possessions than Jacob had.

One day when Esau came home hungry and tired from hunting, he asked for a bowl of Jacob's soup. Jacob answered, "I will give it to you if you first sell me your birthright."

Esau answered, "What is the use of the birthright? I'm almost starving." So he sold it to Jacob for a bowl of soup.

Isaac was now becoming feeble and almost blind. One day he said to Esau, "Go out into the field and hunt for a deer. Make me the dish of meat I like best, and bring it to me. Then I will give you the blessing."

Rebekah was listening, and she wanted Jacob to have the blessing! She dressed Jacob in Esau's clothes and put goat skin on his arms and neck, so Isaac would think it was Esau. Then she sent Jacob into Isaac's tent with the meat she had prepared. Isaac ate it and blessed Jacob instead of Esau.

Rebekah's plot had worked.

Genesis 25:11-34; 26; 27:1-29

Isaac is deceived by Rebekah and Jacob.

Parents: *By faith Isaac blessed Jacob and Esau concerning things to come.* (Hebrews 11:20)

Children:
1. Which of the twins did Rebekah like best?
2. What did Esau sell for a bowl of soup?
3. How did Rebekah and Jacob deceive Isaac?

JACOB FLEES FROM HOME
God Comforts Him in a Dream

After Esau discovered that he had lost his blessing, he was very angry. He said, "Soon my father will die, and then I will kill Jacob."

When Rebekah heard this, she said to Jacob, "Leave home and get out of Esau's sight before it is too late. Perhaps when he no longer sees you, he will forget his anger."

Jacob left home, beginning his long journey alone to Haran. One evening at sunset, he stopped to rest for the night. He took some stones for a pillow and lay down to sleep. That night he had a wonderful dream. He saw stairs leading up to heaven from the earth, and angels were coming down and going up on the stairs. At the top of the stairs, he saw the Lord God standing. The Lord said to Jacob, "The land where you are shall be yours and your children's after you. I will take good care of you, and will bring you back again to this land."

In the morning, Jacob woke and said, "The Lord is in this place, and I did not know it! I thought I was all alone. This place is the house of God; it is the gate of heaven." Jacob made a pillar with the stones he had used for his pillow. He poured oil on it for a thankoffering to God.

Then Jacob journeyed on until at last he came to a well near the city of Haran. While waiting at the well, he met Rachel—his own cousin. He was so glad that he wept for joy.

At that moment Jacob began to love Rachel. He longed to have her for his wife.

Genesis 27:30-46; 28; 29:1-14

Jacob dreams of angels and the Lord God.

Parents: *The angel of the Lord encampeth round about them that fear him, and delivereth them.* (Psalm 34:7)

Children: 1. Why did Jacob leave home?
2. Who went up and down the stairs in Jacob's dream?
3. Who stood at the top of the stairs?
4. What did Jacob use for a pillow?

JACOB DECEIVED, WRESTLES WITH AN ANGEL

A Long, Long Lesson

While Jacob stayed in Haran, he wanted Rachel, the daughter of Laban, for his wife. Jacob told Laban, "I will work for you seven years if you will give me Rachel." Laban agreed.

On the day of the wedding, the bride was brought to Jacob. As was the custom in that land, she was covered with a thick veil so her face could not be seen. They were married, but later when Jacob lifted the veil, he found that he had not married Rachel whom he loved. It was her older sister, Leah, whom he did not love at all!

Jacob was very upset that he had been deceived, though he himself had deceived his father in much the same way. But Laban said, "In our land we do not allow the younger to marry before the older. I will give Rachel to you also if you work for me another seven years." Jacob agreed to this, and Rachel also became his wife.

After serving his uncle Laban for twenty years, Jacob gathered together his family and possessions and left Haran. On the way back to his homeland Canaan, he heard news that filled him with fear. He heard that his brother, Esau, was coming with four hundred men. Jacob remembered that Esau had threatened to kill him.

That night Jacob sent his family across a brook, while he stayed behind to pray. While Jacob was alone, he felt a man take hold of him. Jacob wrestled with this strange man until morning. The man was an angel of God. He blessed Jacob and changed his name to Israel.

When Israel met Esau, they made peace with each other.

Genesis 29:15-35; 30; 31; 32; 33:1-16

Jacob wrestles with an angel and receives God's blessing.

Parents: *The eyes of the Lord are upon the righteous, and his ears are open unto their cry.* (Psalm 34:15)

Children: 1. How did Laban deceive Jacob?
2. With whom did Jacob wrestle?
3. What was Jacob's name changed to?

DREAMS WITH SPECIAL MESSAGES
Joseph is Sold

After Jacob came back to the land of Canaan, his youngest son Benjamin was born. Now Jacob had twelve sons. Of all Jacob's children, Joseph was his favorite. He loved Joseph because he was Rachel's child, and because he was the son of his old age. Joseph was also a good boy, faithful and thoughtful. Jacob made Joseph a special coat, a mark of his favor to Joseph. It made his older brothers very jealous.

One day Joseph said, "Listen to this dream. I dreamed we were out in the field binding sheaves when suddenly my sheaf stood up, and all your sheaves bowed down to my sheaf."

His brothers answered scornfully, "Do you think that you will rule over us, and we will bow down to you?"

A few days later Joseph said, "I have dreamed again. This time I saw the sun and the moon and eleven stars all come and bow down to me."

Now Joseph's brothers hated him more than ever. They would not speak kindly to him. But his father gave much thought to what Joseph had said.

One time Joseph's brothers were taking care of their flocks far away from home. Jacob asked Joseph to go see whether all was well with them.

When Joseph's brothers saw him coming, they said, "Look, here comes the dreamer. Let's kill him." But Reuben pitied Joseph and persuaded the others to put him into a nearby pit instead. He planned to later return Joseph to his father.

While they sat down to eat their dinner, a group of Midianite merchants came down the road. The brothers decided to sell Joseph, their own brother, for twenty pieces of silver. The merchants took Joseph to Egypt. He was very sad.

Then the brothers killed a goat and dipped Joseph's special coat into the blood. When their father Jacob saw the bloody coat, he thought Joseph had been killed by a wild beast. He mourned for Joseph.

Genesis 37

Joseph is sold for twenty pieces of silver.

Parents: *Where envying and strife is, there is confusion and every evil work.* (James 3:16)

Children: 1. Who had a coat of many colors?
2. Why did Joseph's brothers hate him?
3. What did they do with Joseph?

JOSEPH INTERPRETS PHARAOH'S DREAM
From Prison to Palace

After many days, Joseph arrived in Egypt. How strange it must have seemed for him to see the great Nile River and the cities full of people.

The merchants sold Joseph as a slave to Potiphar, an officer in the army of Pharaoh, who was ruler of Egypt. Joseph was a handsome boy, with a pleasant and willing spirit. His master, Potiphar, soon placed Joseph in charge of all his house.

At first Potiphar's wife was very friendly to Joseph. But when Joseph would not do wrong to please her, she became his enemy. She falsely accused Joseph of doing a wicked deed. Potiphar believed her story and had Joseph cast into a dark prison.

Joseph had faith in God. In prison, he was cheerful, kind, and helpful. Soon, because of his faithfulness and honesty, the keeper of the prison put Joseph in charge of all the prisoners.

When Joseph was thirty years old, Pharaoh had a dream that troubled him greatly. One of his servants told him about Joseph.

Immediately Pharaoh called for Joseph and said, "I understand that you can interpret dreams."

Joseph answered, "Of myself I am not able to do it, but God will give Pharaoh a good answer."

Pharaoh said that in his dream seven nice, fat cows came up out of a river. Then seven thin cows ate up the seven fat cows, but they still looked thin, poor, and miserable.

Then Joseph said to the king, "Your dream means there will be seven very good years, followed by seven very poor years. The king should appoint someone to store much food in the seven good years."

Right away the king appointed Joseph and made him the second most powerful ruler in Egypt. God had not forgotten His friend Joseph.

Genesis 39-41

Joseph brings glory to God by interpreting Pharaoh's dream.

Parents: *Blessed is everyone that feareth the Lord; that walketh in his ways.* (Psalm 128:1)

Children:
1. Why did the people like Joseph?
2. Who told Joseph what Pharaoh's dream meant?
3. How did the king reward Joseph?

JOSEPH'S BROTHERS COME TO EGYPT
His Dreams Come True

J oseph was made ruler over the land of Egypt, and did his work faithfully and thoroughly. Seven years of plenty soon slipped by, then began the years of famine. Even in the land of Canaan where Joseph's family lived, food was scarce. His father Jacob heard that there was corn in Egypt and sent Joseph's ten brothers to get some.

When the brothers arrived in Egypt and came before Joseph, they did not realize who he was. But Joseph recognized them. As the brothers bowed before him with their faces to the ground, no doubt Joseph remembered his dreams. He decided to treat his brothers harshly to see if they were still as selfish and cruel as they had been. So he talked sharply to them, as if he were a stranger. He put them all in prison for three days, accusing them of being spies. After this, he kept Simeon in prison while the others went home. Joseph told them not to come back unless Benjamin, their younger brother, came with them.

Soon the corn was gone, and the brothers had no choice but to go to Egypt again. This time they took Benjamin with them. Once more the brothers all bowed to Joseph.

A dinner was prepared for them, and Joseph arranged the seating for his brothers. He placed them all in order, from the oldest to the youngest. The brothers marveled. How could this foreign ruler know the order of their ages?

By this time Joseph's heart was so full that he could not keep back his tears. He hurried to his own room to cry.

After testing his brothers' honesty one more time, Joseph knew they were no longer cruel and selfish. He sent his servants out of the room. He wept aloud and said, "I am Joseph your brother, whom you sold into Egypt!" Joseph, with love and tears of joy, kissed his brothers.

Joseph sent wagons and much food home with his brothers. He told them to bring his father and all his family to live in Egypt.

Genesis 42-46

Joseph reveals himself to his brothers.

Parents: *This is my commandment, That ye love one another, as I have loved you.* (John 15:12)

Children: 1. Did Joseph's dreams come true?
2. Why was Joseph so stern with his brothers?
3. Did Joseph still love his brothers, even if they mistreated him?

MOSES ON THE NILE RIVER
A Basket in the Bulrushes

During Joseph's lifetime, the Egyptians treated the people of Israel kindly. Sometime after Joseph died, a king who cared nothing for Joseph or the Israelites began to rule Egypt.

This king said, "Let us rule these Israelites more strictly and make them work hard for Egypt." He was afraid the Israelites would become too numerous and powerful. He commanded that all the Israelite baby boys be killed.

At this crucial time, a lovely little boy was born to an Israelite family. For a while his mother hid him, but soon she had to make other plans for her active, noisy baby. How could she save him from the Egyptians? Surely God would provide a way.

She made a little *ark*, or basket, from tall weeds that grew by the river. She covered it with pitch to keep out the water. Then she put her baby into the basket and placed it among the bushes at the edge of the river. She also sent her twelve-year-old daughter, Miriam, to watch close by.

Soon Pharaoh's daughter and her maids came down to the river to bathe, and they spotted the basket. The princess sent her maid to get it. When they opened the basket, the little baby began to cry.

"This is an Israelite baby!" the princess exclaimed. She loved him at once.

Then Miriam, who had been watching, asked if she should get a Hebrew woman to nurse the baby. The princess agreed, and Miriam ran to get her mother.

When Miram's mother came, Pharaoh's daughter said, "Take this child and nurse him, and I will pay you for it." So the mother happily took her child home again. There she taught him all the ways of the Lord.

When the child was old enough to leave his mother, the princess took him into her own home in the palace. She named him *Moses*.

Exodus 1; 2:1-10

Pharaoh's daughter discovers baby Moses in a basket.

Parents: *By faith Moses, when he was come to years, refused to be called the son of Pharaoh's daughter, choosing rather to suffer affliction with the people of God, than to enjoy the pleasures of sin for a season.* (Hebrews 11:24-25)

Children: 1. What was the name of the baby who was put in the basket?
2. Why did his mother put him there?
3. Who found the little baby?

THE BURNING BUSH
A Voice in the Desert

Moses grew up among the Egyptians and learned their wisdom. But in his heart he still loved his own people, the Israelites, who were now poor, hated slaves. Yet they served the Lord God, while the Egyptians worshiped idols and animals.

Moses felt a call from God to help the Israelites. When Pharaoh, the ruler of Egypt, heard about his efforts to free them from slavery, he became angry. Moses fled to another country when Pharaoh tried to kill him. There he became a shepherd.

One day Moses saw a strange sight. A bush was burning on the mountainside. Though it kept on burning, it was not destroyed.

As Moses approached the bush, the angel of the Lord appeared in the flame. A voice called, "Moses, do not come near; take off your shoes, for you are standing on holy ground."

Then God told Moses, "Come now, and I will send you to Pharaoh, and you shall lead my people out of Egypt."

Moses replied, "What if the people ask, 'Who is this God? What is His name?' "

God answered Moses, "Say to them, the I AM has sent me, the One who is always living."

But Moses wanted to see a special sign, so God performed two miracles. First, He told Moses to throw his rod on the ground. When Moses obeyed, the rod became a serpent. Next, God allowed Moses' hand to become diseased with leprosy. Then the Lord turned the serpent back into a rod and healed the diseased hand.

Still Moses was unwilling to go, because he thought he could not speak well enough. God answered him, "Am not I the Lord, who made man's mouth? I will teach you what to say." Still Moses hesitated. Then God said that Moses' brother Aaron could be his spokesman. At last Moses yielded to God's call.

God sent Aaron to meet Moses, and together they headed toward Egypt. They gathered the elders of Israel and told them all the Lord had said.

Exodus 2:11-25; 3; 4

God speaks to Moses from a burning bush.

Parents: *Thou shalt go to all that I shall send thee, and whatsoever I command thee thou shalt speak. Be not afraid of their faces: for I am with thee to deliver thee, saith the Lord.* (Jeremiah 1:7b-8)

Children:
1. What did God tell Moses to do when he came near the bush?
2. Why did God want Moses to go back to Egypt?
3. What miracle happened with Moses' rod?

33

MOSES AND AARON SPEAK TO PHARAOH
A Battle Between God and Man

After Moses and Aaron had spoken to the people of Israel, they went to meet Pharaoh, the king of Egypt. They said, "Our God, the Lord God of Israel, is calling us to worship Him. To do this, we and all our people must go on a journey of three days into the wilderness."

Pharaoh became very angry. He said, "Moses and Aaron, what are you doing to call your people away from their work! Go back to your jobs and leave your people alone. I know why the Israelites are talking about going into the wilderness. It is because they are running out of work, so I will give them more work."

At that time the Israelites had been putting up brick buildings for the Egyptian rulers. They had been making their own bricks from clay mixed with straw. Up until then the Egyptians had been providing the straw for making bricks. Now Pharaoh said, "Let them make just as many bricks as before, but give them no straw." Of course this made the Israelites' backbreaking work almost unbearable. How could they ever find and gather enough straw and still make as many bricks each day as before?

The Israelites became angry with Moses and Aaron. "We thought you would set us free, but now our suffering is greater!" they said.

Moses called upon the Lord, and the Lord said, "Go and speak to Pharaoh again and show him the signs I gave you."

Pharaoh scoffed, "Who is the Lord? Why should I obey His commands?"

Then Aaron threw down his rod, and it turned into a serpent. Pharaoh called his magicians. They also turned their rods into serpents. The Lord let them do this, but He caused Aaron's rod, in the form of a serpent, to swallow up the others. Still Pharaoh would not let the children of Israel go.

Exodus 5-7:13

Aaron's rod turns into a serpent and swallows the other serpents.

Parents: *I know that the Lord will maintain the cause of the afflicted, and the right of the poor.* (Psalm 140:12)

Children: 1. What were the Israelites making with clay?
2. Why did their work become harder?
3. Who did Moses call upon for help?

THE PLAGUES
Wonders in Egypt

The Lord told Moses, "Pharaoh has hardened his heart, and he refuses to hear my voice. He will not let my people go. In the morning, go stand by the river. When Pharaoh comes, wave your rod over the waters of Egypt."

Moses and Aaron obeyed the Lord. When Aaron struck the water, it turned into blood. All the fish died and a terrible stench hung over the land.

After seven days the Lord took away the plague of blood, but Pharaoh refused to repent. Next came huge numbers of frogs that covered the land. They were jumping around in the houses and everywhere else. But Pharaoh's heart just became harder.

Then Aaron struck the dust on the ground, and everywhere the dust became alive with lice. The lice crept on the people and the cattle.

Next God sent flies that swarmed into the houses and covered the land. But where the Israelites lived, there were no lice or flies.

Then came a terrible disease that struck all the animals in Egypt. The horses, camels, sheep, and oxen died by the thousands. But no plague came upon the flocks of the Israelites.

After this Moses and Aaron took ashes from the furnace and threw them up like a cloud into the air. Instantly boils began to break out on man and beast. This was followed by a great hailstorm, such as had never happened before in Egypt. Moses and Aaron often pled with Pharaoh, but he would not let Israel go.

After the hailstorm came a strong east wind bringing clouds of locusts. The locusts ate up every green thing the hail had spared. Finally a thick darkness came that stayed for three days. The Egyptians could not see the sun, moon, or stars.

Then Pharaoh shouted at Moses, "Get out of my sight, and let me never see your face again!"

Moses replied, "It shall be as you say."

Exodus 7:14-25; 8; 9; 10

Egypt is destroyed by the plagues.

Parents: *Because sentence against an evil work is not executed speedily, therefore the heart of the sons of men is fully set in them to do evil.* (Ecclesiastes 8:11)

Children:
1. What did the waters of Egypt turn into?
2. How many days was it dark?
3. What did Pharaoh finally tell Moses to do?

THE PASSOVER
Freedom at Last

The Israelites lived in safety under God's care, while the Egyptians suffered destruction from the plagues. By now many of the Egyptians feared the God of the Israelites and Moses, His servant.

Moses said to the people, "God will bring one more plague upon the Egyptians, and then they will let us go. Gather yourselves together in order by your families, and be ready to march out of Egypt. At midnight, the Lord's angel will go through the land and kill the oldest son in every house. But your family shall be safe if you do exactly as I command you."

Every family was told to kill a lamb. They were to sprinkle the lamb's blood at the entrance of the house, on the door frame overhead and on each side. No one was to go out of his house that night, for it was the Lord's passover.

That night a great cry went up over all the land of Egypt. In every house, the oldest son had died. Pharaoh, the king of Egypt, saw his own son lie dead and knew it was the hand of God. All the people of Egypt were filled with terror as they saw their children dead in their houses.

The king now sent a messenger to Moses, saying, "Hurry and get out of the land. Take everything you have and leave nothing. Pray to your God to have mercy on us."

Early in the morning, the Israelites left Egypt after living there four hundred years.

The Lord God went before the large group of people. During the daytime He formed a great cloud, like a pillar, in front of them. At night it became a pillar of fire. It guided them by day and gave light by night.

Exodus 12-13

The blood of a lamb protects the obedient from death.

Parents: *Christ our passover is sacrificed for us.* (1 Corinthians 5:7b)

Children:
1. What did the Israelites put on the door top and sides?
2. Why did they do this?
3. Who was to pass through at midnight?

THE RED SEA IS DIVIDED
Led by Pillar of Cloud and Fire

The children of Israel traveled toward the Red Sea, led by the pillar of cloud and fire. In a few days they came to the seashore, with the water before them and high mountains on each side. But King Pharaoh wanted them back as soon as they had gone. He called out his army, his chariots, and his horsemen, and followed them. Very soon the army of Egypt was behind the Israelites.

The people shook with fear and cried to Moses, "Why did you bring us out to this terrible place? It would be better to serve the Egyptians than to die here in the wilderness!"

"Do not be afraid," answered Moses. "Stand still, and see how God will save you. The Lord will fight for you, and you will never see the Egyptians again."

Then the pillar of cloud went behind them and stood between the Egyptians and the Israelites. To the Israelites it was bright with the glory of the Lord, but to the Egyptians it was dark and terrible.

All that night a mighty east wind blew over the sea. By morning there was a path of dry land with walls of water on either side. Then the pillar of cloud went before them. The Israelites walked safely through the sea and into the wilderness on the other side.

The Egyptians followed with their chariots and horses. But the Lord slowed them by taking off their chariot wheels.

By this time all the Israelites had passed through. Then Moses stretched out his hand over the sea, and the walls of water rushed back together again. All the army of Pharaoh drowned in the sea, before the eyes of the children of Israel.

Then Moses wrote a song of victory, and all the people sang it together.

Exodus 14-15

The Egyptian army is destroyed by God's wrath.

Parents: *By faith they passed through the Red Sea as by dry land: which the Egyptians assaying to do were drowned.* (Hebrews 11:29)

Children:
1. How did the people know where to go?
2. Who made the cloud move?
3. What happened to Pharaoh's army?

NEW TESTAMENT

Table of Contents

THE ANGEL GABRIEL VISITS MARY
A Saviour Will Be Born

What is more tiresome than a dark night when you are not feeling well and cannot sleep? The night hours pass so slowly. At last you see the first sunbeams of the morning. The birds begin to sing, and everything seems to brighten.

The state of the world before Jesus came was like a long, dark night. Israel's prophets wrote that the people walked in darkness. The wonderful light of God's Son would brighten the dark, sinful world.

For a long time nobody knew just when or where the Saviour would be born. Eve, the first mother, was hoping her son might be the appointed one. Moses declared that God would raise unto the people a prophet like himself. Many years later Isaiah prophesied that a virgin would bear a son. Still later the prophet Micah revealed the very town where the child would be born.

Yet nothing happened. As the years rolled by, the prophecies were gradually forgotten. There was no message from heaven for over four hundred years.

But God knew just the right time to fulfill all the prophecies. He sent the angel Gabriel to the earth with a message for a virgin named Mary.

Gabriel knew the city, the right house, and even the very room where he would find Mary. He entered and said, "Hail, Mary, you are highly favored. The Lord is with you."

Mary was frightened by her heavenly visitor. But Gabriel said, "Don't be afraid, Mary. You are going to have a Son. He will be very special. He will be called the Son of the Highest, whose kingdom will last forever."

"How can such a thing happen to me?" Mary asked in wonder. "I am not yet married."

Gabriel answered, "The Holy Spirit will come upon you and God's power will rest on you. That is why your child will be God's own Son. Nothing is too hard for God."

"I really don't understand," said Mary quietly, "but I am God's servant. I am ready to do anything He asks me to do."

Luke 1:26-38

The angel Gabriel tells Mary she will have a Son.

Parents: *. . . Behold, a virgin shall conceive, and bear a son, and shall call his name Immanuel.* (Isaiah 7:14)

Children: 1. Who sent the angel to Mary?
                2. Was Mary afraid when she saw the angel?
                3. Who would Mary's Son be?

JESUS IS BORN IN BETHLEHEM
No Room in the Inn

One of the greatest events of all time was about to happen! Jesus would be born to the virgin Mary. He would be called the Son of the Highest.

Before Jesus was born, Mary visited her cousin Elisabeth. She stayed three months before returning to her home in Nazareth. There Joseph waited, eagerly looking forward to their wedding day. When Mary said she would have a baby, Joseph was shocked. He thought Mary had been unfaithful to him.

Mary told Joseph about her heavenly visitor. Still he doubted. Had she really seen an angel? Was this baby to be God's Son? Was Mary telling the truth?

Joseph decided to break off the marriage as quietly as possible. He did not want Mary to be shamed and publicly disgraced.

But God knew his thoughts. That very night He sent His angel Gabriel to Joseph in a dream. "Don't be upset," he said, "Mary's baby will be born through God's power and His Spirit. You shall name Him *Jesus*, for He shall save His people from their sins." How relieved Joseph felt to hear this message. Gladly he took Mary as his wife.

Then came the news from the Roman emperor that all the people would be taxed, and everyone must register at his home town. For Joseph this meant going to Bethlehem. He took Mary on the tiresome four-day journey to Bethlehem.

When they arrived, Mary longed for a soft bed. But alas, the inn at Bethlehem was already full. So they had to stay in a stable. There Mary's baby was born.

Joseph and Mary gazed with joy at the little child. This was the promised Messiah! Joseph said, "We shall name Him *Jesus*, just like the angel told me. He is the one God sent to save us."

Mary wrapped baby Jesus in long strips of cloth, then Joseph laid Him in a manger.

Matthew 1:18-25
Luke 2:1-7

Baby Jesus is born in a stable.

Parents: *For unto us a child is born, unto us a son is given.* (Isaiah 9:6)

Children: 1. Who told Joseph to name the baby *Jesus*?
2. In what city was Jesus born?
3. Where did they lay Jesus?

THE SHEPHERDS AND THE WISE MEN
Heavenly Messengers Announce the Good News

A few hours after Jesus was born, Bethlehem became very quiet. Far away a dog barked. The sleeping town had no idea that a great event had just taken place. Out on a hillside nearby, some shepherds huddled sleepily near their flocks.

Suddenly a glorious light shone round about them, and an angel appeared. The shepherds were terrified.

"Don't be afraid, for I am bringing you the most joyful news you could hear," the angel said. "Christ the Saviour is born in a stable in Bethlehem. You will find Him wrapped in long strips of cloth, lying in a manger."

At once the whole countryside lit up with glory as thousands of angels appeared. Their musical voices rose in a chorus of praise. "Glory to God in the highest, and on earth peace, good will to men." Then the angels vanished as suddenly as they had come.

The shepherds hurried across the hills and valleys to Bethlehem. There they found the baby Jesus just as the angel had said. They told Joseph and Mary all about the angels.

Finally the shepherds returned to their flocks. They told the wonderful news to everyone they met. How they praised God!

Many miles away, some wise men from the east saw a very bright star one night. They decided this was a sign from God, meaning that a new king had been born. Quickly they loaded their camels and traveled to the land of Israel.

At Jerusalem, the wise men asked, "Where is the newborn king of the Jews?" Herod directed them to Bethlehem. That night the bright star moved toward Bethlehem. It led the men right to the house where Jesus was.

How glad the wise men were to find Jesus! They knelt down and worshiped the baby king. Then they gave Him gifts of gold, frankincense, and myrrh. Perhaps this was God's way of providing for His faithful servants, Joseph and Mary.

Luke 2:8-20
Matthew 2:1-12

The shepherds listen to the angel's good news.

Parents: *For God so loved the world, that he gave his only begotten Son, that whosoever believeth in him should not perish, but have everlasting life.* (John 3:16)

Children: 1. Why were the shepherds outside at night?
2. Who told the shepherds that Jesus was born?
3. What guided the wise men to the baby Jesus?

JESUS TEACHES LOVE AND FORGIVENESS
Lost Sheep and an Ungrateful Servant

One day some Pharisees, scribes, and lawyers came to listen to Jesus. They were shocked to see thieves, liars, crooks, and immoral people with Him. "Jesus should not let these sinners mix with the 'respectable' Jews," they complained. "Neither should He eat with them."

Jesus heard their grumbling. He told them, "Imagine that you owned one hundred sheep. One night you notice that one lamb is missing. Would you go to bed thinking that one lost lamb doesn't matter? Of course not! No matter how tired you would be, you would search diligently until you found it. Then you would gladly bring it back to the sheepfold. You would invite your neighbors to rejoice with you, because your lost lamb has been found."

Jesus continued, "That is the way God feels about people. There is more joy in heaven over one sinner who humbly comes to God than over ninety-nine people who already obey Him."

Peter also needed to learn about how God deals with people. One day he asked, "Master, how many times should I forgive someone who keeps mistreating me? Is seven times enough?"

"No, Peter," answered Jesus. "Keep on forgiving until seventy times seven. Listen to this parable."

A certain king found out that one of his servants owed him millions of dollars. He commanded that this man, his wife, and his children, should all be sold as slaves. But the servant fell on his knees and begged the king for mercy. The king pitied the man and erased the debt from his records.

The servant went outside and found another servant who owed him a few dollars. Grabbing him by the neck, he demanded, "Pay me at once!"

"Please be patient and I'll pay you," the servant begged. But the first servant would not listen. He had the poor man cast into prison.

When the king heard this, he was furious. He told the wicked servant, "I forgave you millions of dollars, yet you refuse to forgive only a few dollars. Because of this, you must go to prison until you pay me everything."

"Remember," said Jesus, "God will not forgive you unless you forgive one another with your whole heart."

Matthew 18:7-14, 21-35
Luke 15:3-7

The shepherd joyfully brings back his lost lamb.

Parents: *The Son of man is come to save that which was lost.*
(Matthew 18:11)

Children: 1. Why would the shepherd leave his 99 sheep?
2. How often does God want us to forgive someone?
3. Will God forgive us if we don't forgive others?

51

JESUS IS CRUCIFIED
A Great Day of Suffering

Pilate did not know what to do. He did not want to condemn an innocent man. Besides, his own wife had sent him this message: *Leave that righteous man alone. This morning I have suffered much pain in a dream because of Him.*

But the angry mob kept roaring, "Crucify Him! Crucify Him!" Soon they all began to shout, "Set Barabbas free!" These Jews did not really care about Barabbas, who was a convicted criminal. But they knew that Pilate usually freed one prisoner during this time. They would free anyone else, even a murderer, rather than Jesus.

Nervously Pilate washed his hands before the crowd. He said, "I am not responsible for this man's death." Yet he tried once more to save Jesus. He ordered his soldiers to whip Jesus severely. Then they forced a crown of thorns on His head, dressed Him in a purple robe, and placed a stick (a mock scepter) in His right hand. Surely now the Jews would pity Jesus when they saw His bloody face and clothes. Pilate brought Him before them and said, "Behold the man!"

But the mob only became louder. "Away with Him! Crucify Him!"

At last Pilate gave up. He freed Barabbas, and allowed them to take Jesus out of the city to a place called Golgotha. There He was nailed to a cross. Though Jesus was in agony, He did not hate His enemies. He prayed, "Father, forgive them for they do not know what they are doing."

Two thieves were also crucified that day, one on either side of Jesus. One of them taunted, "If you are Christ, save yourself and us also!"

But the other thief said, "We deserve to die, but this man is innocent." Turning to Jesus he pleaded, "When you come into your kingdom, remember me."

Immediately Jesus answered, "You will be with me in paradise this very day!"

At noon, the whole world was plunged into darkness. Jesus kept on suffering for three more lonely hours. Just before He died, He gave a shout of victory. "It is finished!" His work on earth was done. Now He could free the whole world from the grip of sin and Satan.

Suddenly the earth shook, rocks split apart, and many graves were opened. The frightened centurion exclaimed, "Surely this was the Son of God!"

Matthew 27:1-54
Mark 15:1-39
Luke 23:1-47
John 18:28-40; 19:1-30

Jesus is crucified between two thieves.

Parents: *. . . the blood of Jesus Christ his Son cleanseth us from all sin.*
(1 John 1:7)

Children: 1. Where was Jesus taken to be crucified?
2. How many men were crucified?
3. Why did Jesus die?

JESUS IS RISEN!
A Glorious Morning

Jesus' faithful friends watched the crucifixion from a distance. In helpless misery, they listened hour after hour to His cries. It was heartbreaking to watch their beloved Master die! Surely that day, as God's wrath against sin was poured on His own perfect Son, had been the harshest hour in human history.

Could it be that only this week Jesus had triumphantly ridden into Jerusalem before cheering crowds? Now, within twenty-four hours, He had been betrayed, tried, condemned, and crucified. To Jesus' followers, life seemed hopeless.

Late on the afternoon of the crucifixion, two honorable men named Joseph and Nicodemus came to the cross. They had not been following Jesus openly because they were afraid of the Jewish leaders. These men who loved Jesus pulled out the nails that had been driven into His hands and feet by men who hated Him. They wrapped His body in linens fragrant with sweet spices. Then they laid Him in a new tomb.

The next day some priests and Pharisees went to Pilate. They said, "This deceiver once said that in three days He would rise again. Now issue an order to have the tomb guarded. Otherwise His disciples may come and steal the body, claiming that He arose from the dead. That would be the worst deception of all!" So Pilate commanded that the tomb must be guarded day and night.

Very early the next morning, a great earthquake shook the tomb. A blinding light flashed on the sleepy soldiers standing guard. It was an angel from heaven, with a face like lightning and a robe as white as snow. The terror-stricken guards shook like leaves before him, completely helpless. In power and great glory, Jesus rose from the dead. The angel rolled the huge stone away from the entrance and sat on it.

Meanwhile, Mary Magdalene, Mary the mother of James, and other women were coming toward the tomb. They were frightened when they saw the angel. But he said kindly, "Do not fear. I know you are looking for Jesus, who was crucified. He is not here, for He is risen! Go quickly and tell His disciples."

The women fled from the tomb, trembling and speechless. Their hearts were filled with fear and great joy.

Matthew 27:55-66; 28:1-10
Mark 16:1-14
Luke 24:1-49
John 20:1-23

The women are astonished to see an angel in the tomb.

Parents: *[He was] declared to be the Son of God with power, according to the spirit of holiness, by the resurrection from the dead.* (Romans 1:4)

Children: 1. Who guarded the tomb?
2. Who rolled away the stone?
3. What did the angel say to the women?

The Way to God and Peace

We live in a world contaminated by sin. Sin is anything that goes against God's holy standards. When we do not follow the guidelines that God our Creator gave us, we are guilty of sin. Sin separates us from God, the source of life.

Since the time when the first man and woman, Adam and Eve, sinned in the Garden of Eden, sin has been universal. The Bible says that we all have "sinned and come short of the glory of God" (Romans 3:23). It also says that the natural consequence for that sin is eternal death, or punishment in an eternal hell: "Then when lust hath conceived, it bringeth forth sin: and sin, when it is finished, bringeth forth death" (James 1:15).

But we do not have to suffer eternal death in hell. God provided forgiveness for our sins through the death of His only Son, Jesus Christ. Because Jesus was perfect and without sin, He could die in our place. "For God so loved the world that he gave his only begotten Son, that whosoever believeth in him should not perish, but have everlasting life" (John 3:16).

A sacrifice is something given to benefit someone else. It costs the giver greatly. Jesus was God's sacrifice. Jesus' death takes away the penalty of sin for everyone who accepts this sacrifice and truly repents of their sins. To repent of sins means to be truly sorry for and turn away from the things we have done that have violated God's standards (Acts 2:38; 3:19).

Jesus died, but He did not remain dead. After three days, God's Spirit miraculously raised Him to life again. God's Spirit does something similar in us. When we receive Jesus as our sacrifice and repent of our sins, our hearts are changed. We become spiritually alive! We develop new desires and attitudes (2 Corinthians 5:17). We begin to make choices that please God (1 John 3:9). If we do fail and commit sins, we can ask God for forgiveness. "If we confess our sins, he is faithful and just to forgive us our sins, and to cleanse us from all unrighteousness" (1 John 1:9).

Once our hearts have been changed, we want to continue growing spiritually. We will be happy to let Jesus be the Master of our lives and will want to become more like Him. To do this, we must meditate on God's Word and commune with God in prayer. We will testify to others of this change by being baptized and sharing the good news of God's victory over sin and death. Fellowship with a faithful group of believers will strengthen our walk with God (1 John 1:7).